www.phaelos.com

FIRST EDITION

Designed by Adam Abraham
Illustrations by Marie Litster
Printed in Korea

Library of Congress Cataloguing-in-Publication Data

Abraham, Adam, 1951 –

 I Am My Body, NOT! / Adam Abraham.

  p. ; cm.

 Illustrated.

 ISBN: 0-9700209-1-0

 1. Child development. 2. Spirituality. 3. Anatomy. 4. Self-awareness I. Title.

11996442   00-104193

PHAELOS

Dedication

This book is dedicated to our children, parents, family and friends.

It is also dedicated to the child in each of us that wonders and questions innocently, who motivates us to harmlessly seek wisdom, knowledge and understanding for the power and freedom that it confers, that together we might look beyond the issue of race, color, and "differentness" and come together from the heart, character, and highest spirit that lives within us all.

Adam Abraham & Marie Litster

How to Use the Vocabulary Power Builder™

Whether you are a parent, teacher, or young reader, you will find the Vocabulary Power Builder that we've developed, a valuable aid to reading comprehension that enhances word and language understanding. Here's how to use it:

1. As you read along you'll notice text labeled in green indicates that its definition has been included in the glossary in the back of the book.

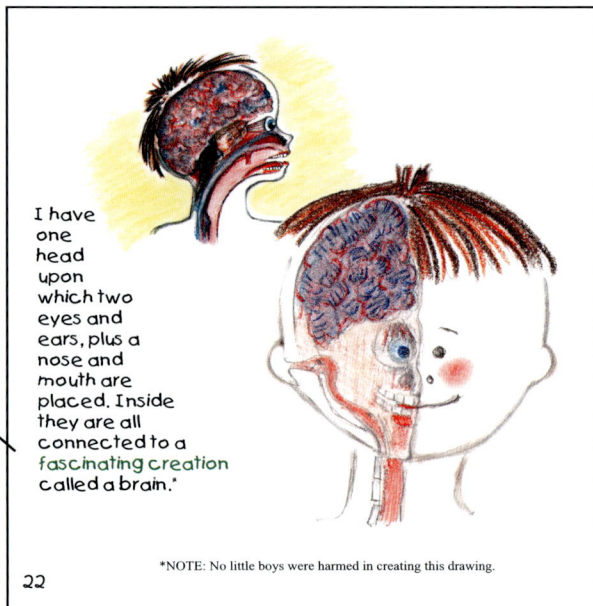

I have one head upon which two eyes and ears, plus a nose and mouth are placed. Inside they are all connected to a fascinating creation called a brain.*

22

*NOTE: No little boys were harmed in creating this drawing.

Data (p. 37) *n.*: another word for information used as a basis for reasoning, discussion, or calculation... to make choices.

Design (p. 37) *v.*: to create, fashion, execute, or construct according to a plan; to devise for a specific function or end.

Different (p. 20) *adj.*: partly or totally unlike in nature, form, or quality; dissimilar; not the same as.

Differentiate (p. 36) *v.*: to mark or show a difference in; constitute a difference that distinguishes; to recognize or give expression to a difference.

Digestive System (p. 28) *n.*: bodily organs (i.e., mouth, throat, stomach, intestines, bowels, etc.) designed to work together to aid digestion, especially of food.

Emotional (p. 38) *adj.*: relating to the expression of human feelings or sensibilities, such as joy, fear, happiness, sadness, etc.

Energy (p. 43) *n.*: power, motivated force; as expressed in electromagnetic waves.

Environment (p. 37) *n.*: the circumstances, objects, or conditions by which one is surrounded; one's personal world or reality, as well as the collective world, or reality.

Essential (p. 29) *adj.*: of the utmost importance; important. Synonym: Fundamental.

Exist (p. 42) *v.*: of or pertaining to being; to have real being whether material or spiritual; to continue to be.

Fascinating (p. 22) *adj.*: commanding the interest of; compelling.

Fiber-optics (p. 25) *n.*: thin transparent fibers of glass or plastic through which light passes for the purposes of lightning fast communication.

Fluid (p. 32) *n.*: a substance that tends to flow by nature; viscous.

48

2. You can then look up the definition of the highlighted word, opening more discussion and possible understanding by youngsters. It's that simple.

I Am My Body, NOT!

Two hands have I, each with four fingers and a thumb.

I use my hands to touch and to hold things.

To put things together and take them apart.

To enjoy the soft, smooth, silky feel of Gingercat's fur.

To grip a hammer so
that I can drive a nail
into the wall and
hang a picture of
Dogwood.

"DOGWOOD"

To tell when the bath water is just the right
temperature for the rest of my body.

As much as
my hands
help me, and
help me to
help my
family,
friends, and
others, they
are not my
body.

And my body
is not me.

7

Two arms have I, one for each hand.

They work together as a whole to let me stretch so that my hands can reach over there.

To pick up that shiny coin I saw on the ground.

To tuck in the label under David's collar.

To give mommy and daddy a great big hug!

If my arms were longer, I'd be able to hug more people at the same time, although if they were too long, they might be too heavy to lift.

I think I'm glad
my arms are
just the way
they are.

14

But as much as my arms help me, and help me to help my family, friends, and others, they are not my body.

And my body is not me.

15

Two legs have I, upon which
I stand, and walk, and run,
and go.

They
help me
to get
here
and
there,
to lift
and
carry
this and
that.

And to be where I need to be.

To each leg a foot is attached, which makes balance an easier proposition.

Without them life would be very... different.

But as much as my legs and feet help me to help my family, friends, and others, they are not my body either.

And my body is not me.

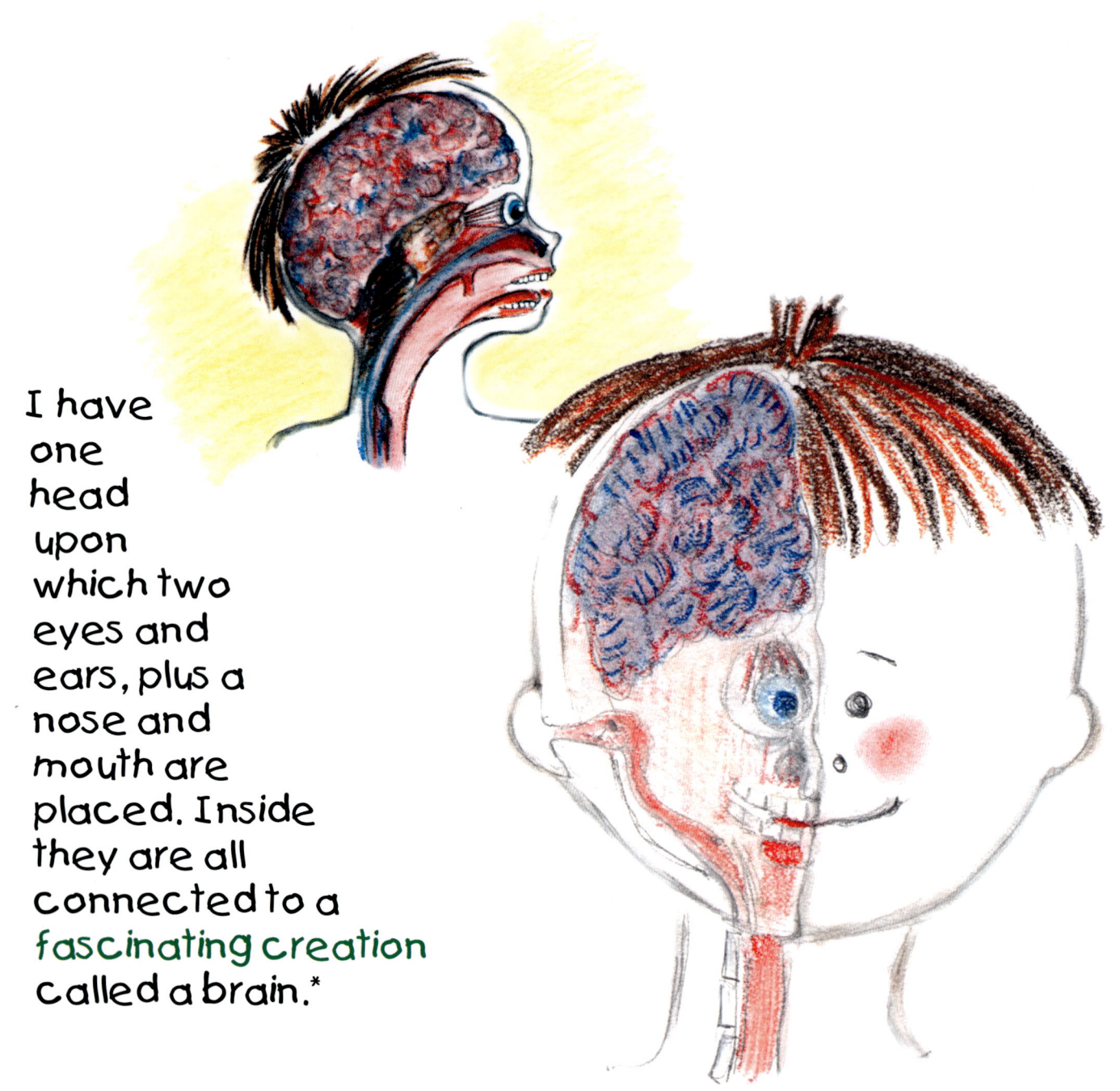

I have
one
head
upon
which two
eyes and
ears, plus a
nose and
mouth are
placed. Inside
they are all
connected to a
fascinating creation
called a brain.*

*NOTE: No little boys were harmed in creating this drawing.

The brain is the "center" of my senses. It "processes" my thoughts and feelings of the world around me. Upon receiving sensations created by the brain, I interpret their meaning. I respond by choosing to act in certain ways.

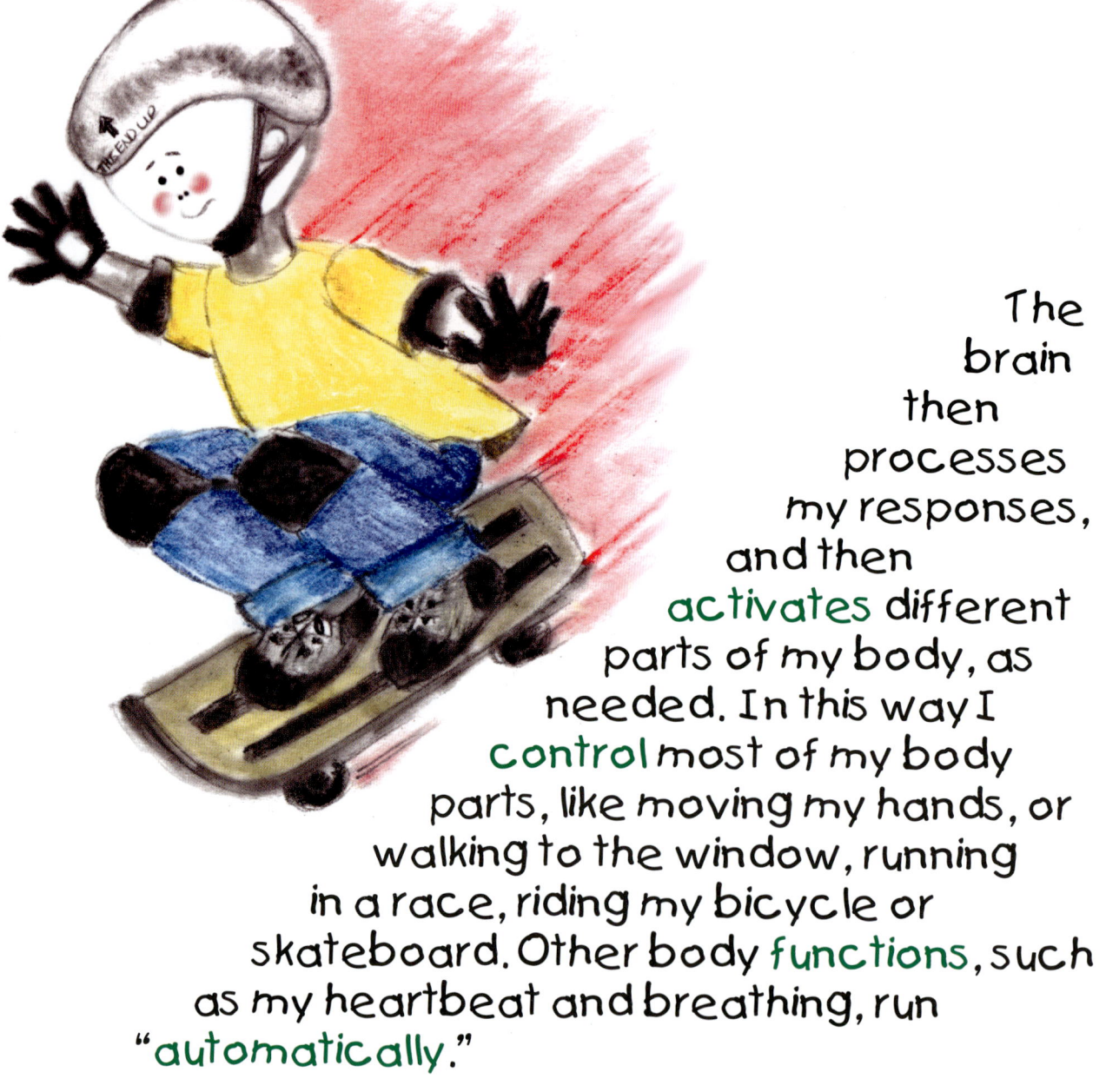

The
brain
then
processes
my responses,
and then
activates different
parts of my body, as
needed. In this way I
control most of my body
parts, like moving my hands, or
walking to the window, running
in a race, riding my bicycle or
skateboard. Other body functions, such
as my heartbeat and breathing, run
"automatically."

24

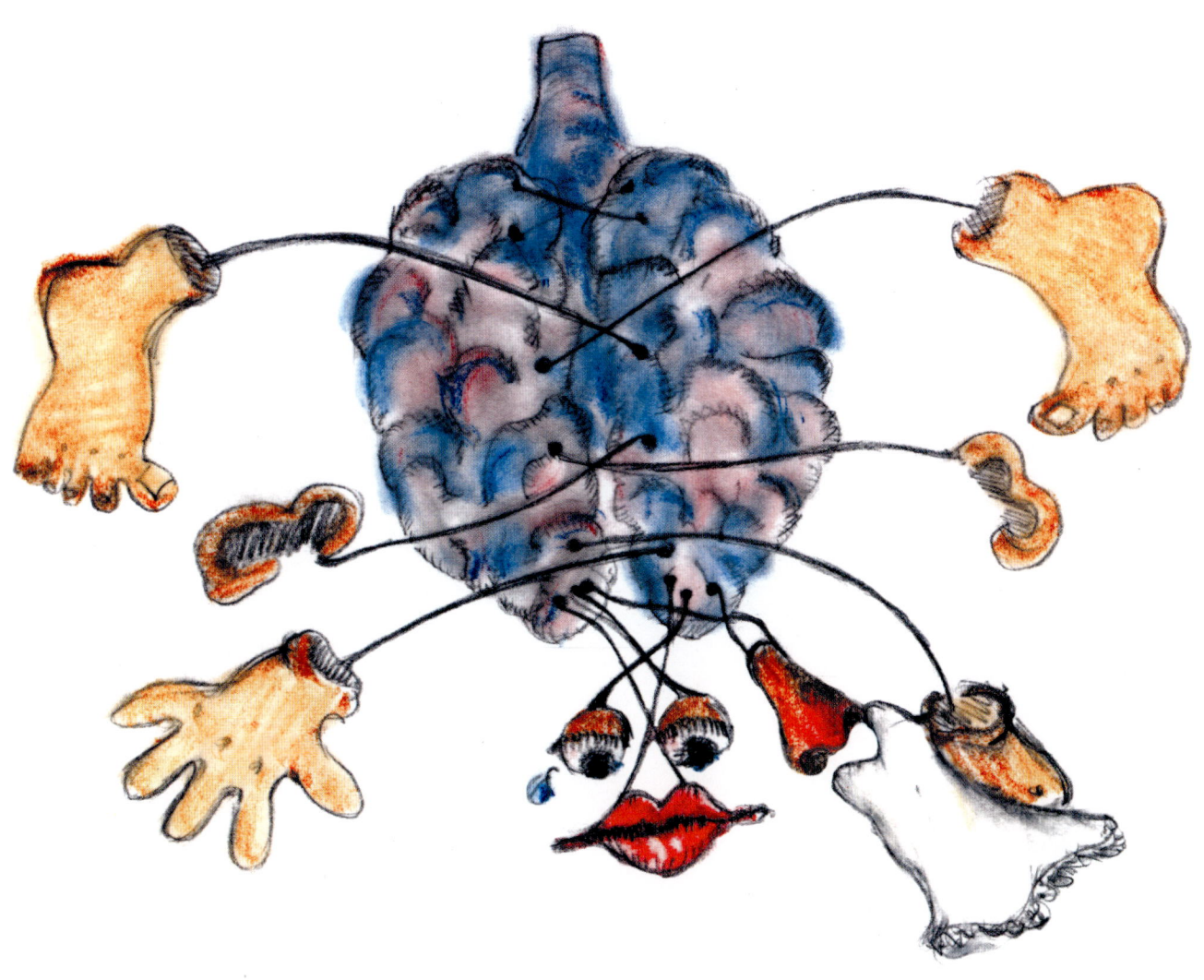

Every part of my body is connected to the brain through a fiber optic-like "network" of tissues called the nervous system.

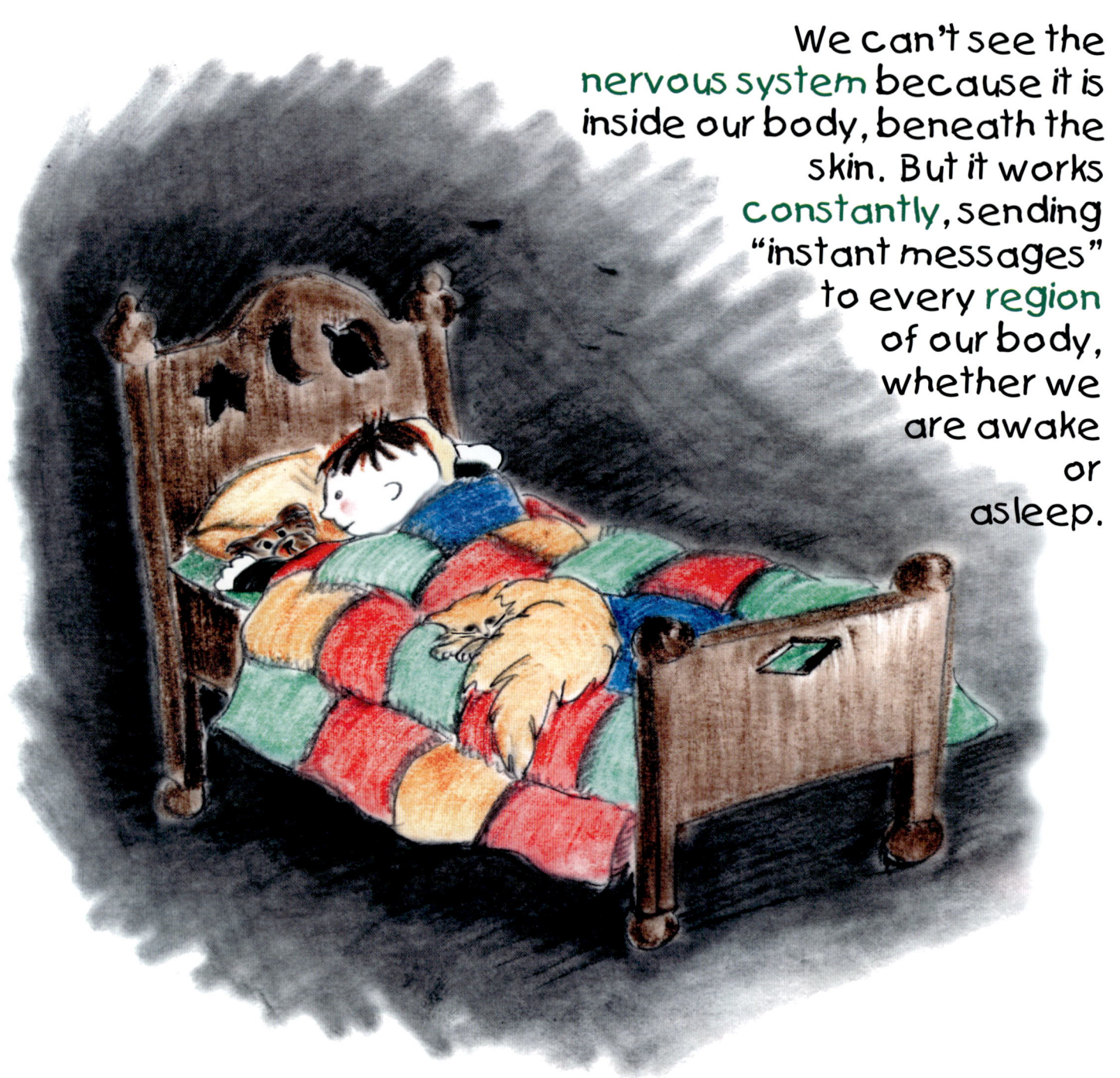

We can't see the nervous system because it is inside our body, beneath the skin. But it works constantly, sending "instant messages" to every region of our body, whether we are awake or asleep.

Even while we sleep, we are monitoring the nervous system, and can awaken at the slightest sign of trouble. Though I have a nervous system, it doesn't mean that I am nervous. Calm people have nervous systems too.

At the center of my body is the torso. It is like a "trunk" that is not a suitcase, which stores and protects vital organs that help make up the core of the "me" that you talk to and see, possible. My legs, arms, and head are connected to mighty muscles such as the heart and lungs.

The torso also holds my digestive system, which includes my stomach, and is the "seat" of the biggest, most comfortable muscle of all, the gluteus maximus, my butt, which along with the upper muscles of my legs, helps to support me when I sit erect.

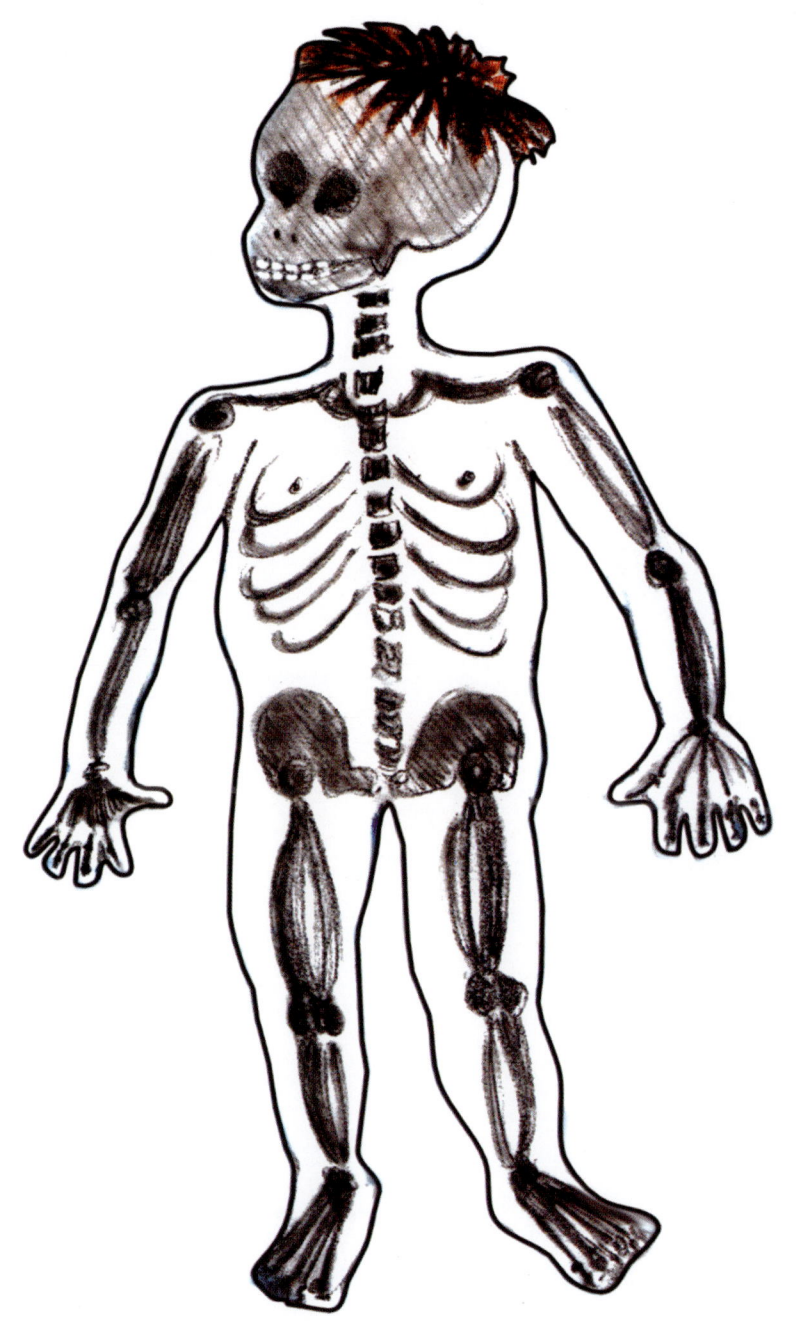

Inside my body, through all its connections is a skeleton, which looks scary by itself without my muscles and tissue, but is essential because it gives my body both support and strength.

Without it I would be unable to stand or sit erect, or roll over, or do headstands or somersaults.

Without a skeleton, I would look like a collapsed blob of muscle tissue and skin that would be barely able to move, except maybe like a snail. But even that would not be me.

Also running through my body is a network of hose-like tissues called the circulatory system. The tissues that make up the circulatory system are called arteries, veins, and capillaries.

This system transports a vital fluid called blood – pumped by the heart – to every part of my body.

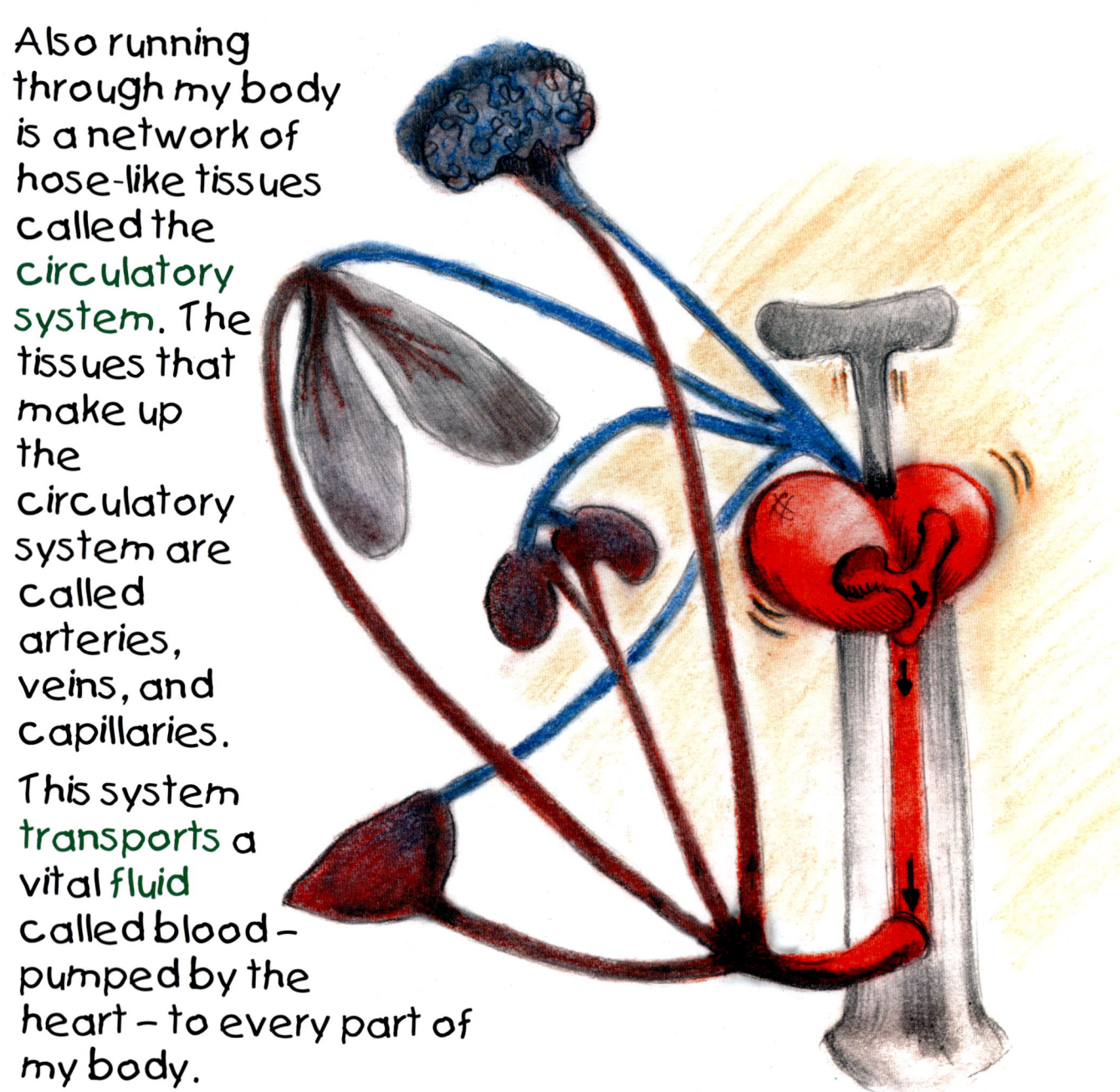

The
main
ingredient
of blood is
water; which
my body cannot
live without. If it
springs a leak that
cannot be healed,
and the blood loss
cannot be stopped
quickly, my body could die.

And though the trunk and skeleton, and brain are all very helpful; though the nervous and circulatory systems are important, and my supply of blood is essential, they are not my body.

And my body is not me.

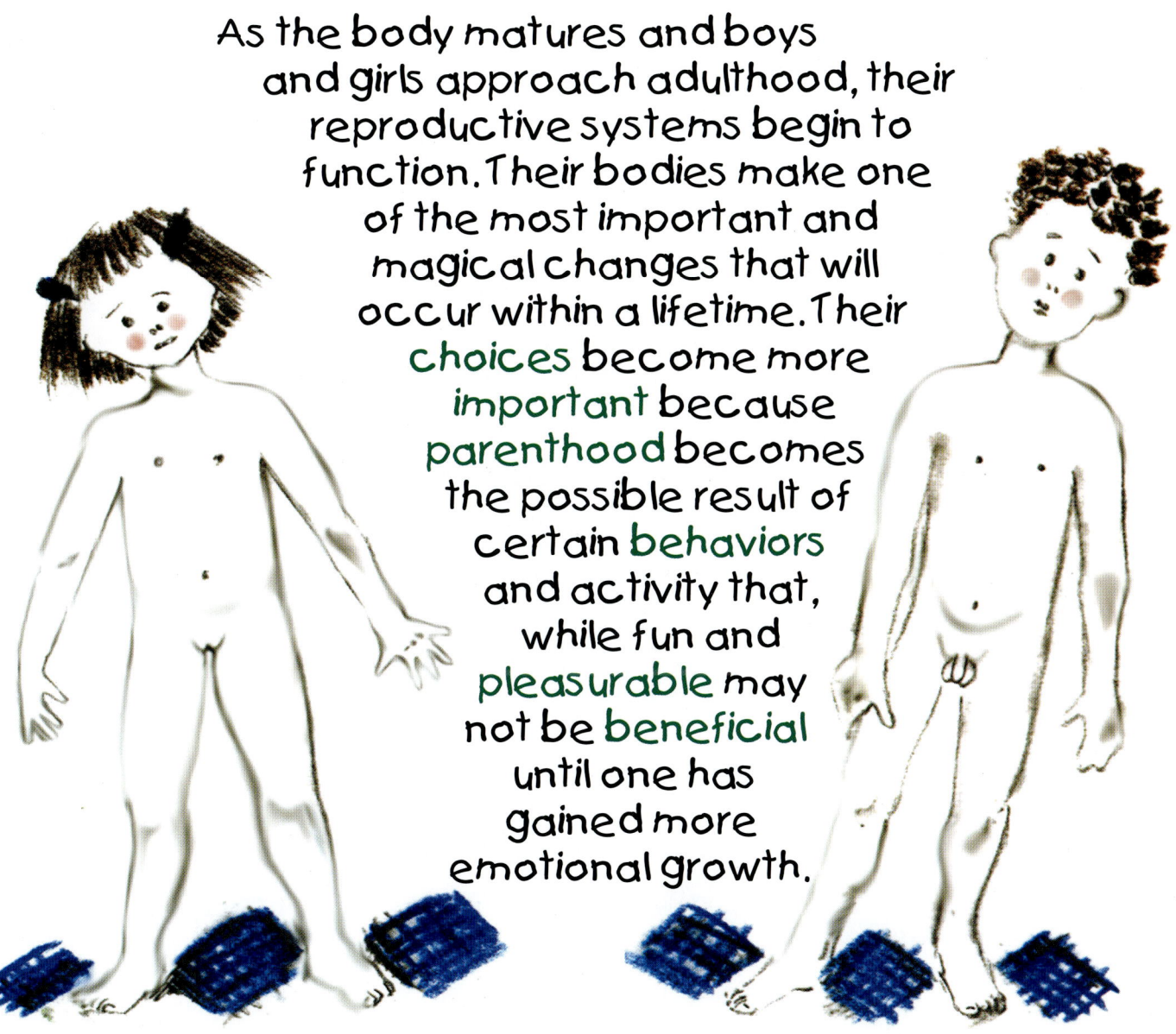

As the body matures and boys and girls approach adulthood, their reproductive systems begin to function. Their bodies make one of the most important and magical changes that will occur within a lifetime. Their choices become more important because parenthood becomes the possible result of certain behaviors and activity that, while fun and pleasurable may not be beneficial until one has gained more emotional growth.

Covering all the pieces that do indeed make up my body, is a very special tissue called skin. It comes in many shades, from very light in tone to very dark. Some people identify themselves and differentiate others by measuring the "shading" of their skin instead of measuring the goodness of their spirit.

The skin serves a vital purpose in the body's design. Its entire surface is a sensor, which constantly provides us data on the status and condition of our environment.

Through
our skin we
are able to know
the status of an area that
is smaller than the size of a
pinhead. By sending pain alarms
in certain situations we get into,
we are guided away from brushes
with further danger. By sending pleasure
signals in other situations, we are guided
toward behaviors that may benefit our
emotional and spiritual health through loving
relationships with others.

My skin is a wondrous instrument; pliable, comfortable, and accommodating, as my size and shape changes throughout the many stages of my life. Self-healing and forgiving, it sets a wonderful example of how I should be toward others, and myself. But as wonderful as my skin is, it is not my body. And my body is not me.

My body is my friend, and in a way of speaking, my servant. If I take care of it, I will most likely enjoy better health. Without it, I cannot be here.

But it is not me.

My body is designed to carry me through the adventure that we call life on earth. It allows me to learn, and build and live in the earthly environment we call home. Through it I make choices and take actions that have impact and meaning.

My body is the instrument by and through which I exist on planet Earth. But it is not me. It is made up of earthly materials. I am not. One day my body will cease to function, thus ending my "stay" on earth, but not my existence, for I am my body, NOT!

I am energy...I am...

Where we go or what we do after our bodies die is anyone's guess. No one knows for sure, though we all believe something. Even a belief in nothingness after a body's death is a belief, and nothing more.

The only ones to whom our choices, attitudes, and behaviors on earth are really relevant, are us and those that we touch during the course of our lives. We are therefore obliged to treat our bodies and each other with love for the betterment of life on earth, and the good that we may share.

What is PHAELOS?

PHAELOS (fy-los) is derived from the Greek, *philos* that means fondness, and loving. Phaelos is a natural quality and expression of humanity that we believe is not necessarily in short supply, but under-utilized in our society.

Phaelos, Inc. was inspired by a vision of, and desire for a better world made possible by *conscious,* loving choice — one mind and heart at a time — through self-reliance and positive cooperation among people.

Vocabulary Power Builder™

Vocabulary is power! It's better to know the meaning of too many words than to know the meaning of too few.

For those of you who are reading some words in *I Am My Body, NOT!* for the first time, we've included a list, along with a page reference and their definitions. Please remember that there may be other meanings of these words. We have included only the meaning of the word as used in this book.

Accommodating (p. 39) *adj.*: to be considerate, adaptable; to bring into agreement or accord.

Activates (p. 24) *v.*: to make something that is static or at rest, active, or in motion.

Adventure (p. 41) *n.*: an exciting or remarkable experience, which sometimes involves great risk, but also, great reward.

Attitudes (p. 44) *n.*: a mental "position" that one assumes about another person, place or thing. Can be "positive" or "negative" in orientation.

Automatically (p. 24) *adj.*: acting or done spontaneously or unconsciously; "on its own."

Balance (p. 19) *n.*: the ability to keep things, including one's self and ideas, upright and steady, and from falling. A state of physical, emotional, mental or spiritual equilibrium.

Behaviors (p. 35) *n.*: a manner of conducting one's self. anything that individuals or groups do involving action and response to stimulation.

Belief (p. 44) *n.*: a state or habit of mind in which trust or confidence is placed in some person, thing, idea, or concept. Synonym: Faith.

Beneficial (p.35) *adj.*: conducive to personal or social well-being, advantage or gain; good.

Betterment (p. 44) *n.*: toward the making or causing something to be better. Synonym: Improvement.

Cease (p. 42) *v.*: to stop, or end, as in activity, function, or existence.

Choices (p. 35) *n.*: the name given to the results of our decisions to favor one way or method of acting and behaving, over another.

Circulatory System (p. 32) *n.*: the system of blood, blood vessels, lymphatics, and heart concerned with the circulation of the blood and lymph.

Constantly (p. 26) *adj.*: continually occurring or recurring.

Collapsed (p. 31) *adj.*: folded down in a more compact shape.

Comfortable (p. 28) *adj.*: affording or enjoying contentment and security; free from stress or tension.

Control (p. 24) *v.*: to exercise restraining or directing influence over; to have power over.

Core (p. 28) *n.*: refers to a central and often foundational part usually distinct from the enveloping part by a difference in nature; the inmost or most intimate part.

Creation (p. 22) *n.*: Something that is or has been made. The result of creating.

Danger (p. 38) *n.*: A state of condition in which one can be hurt or injured or suffer loss or harm.

Data (p. 37) *n.*: Another word for information used as a basis for reasoning, discussion, or calculation… to make choices.

Design (p. 37) *v.*: to create, fashion, execute, or construct according to plan; to devise for a specific function or end.

Different (p. 20) *adj.*: partly or totally unlike in nature, form, or quality; dissimilar; not the same as.

Differentiate (p. 36) *v.*: to mark or show a difference in **:** constitute a difference that distinguishes; to recognize or give expression to a difference.

Digestive System (p. 28) *n.*: bodily organs (i.e., mouth, throat, stomach, intestines, bowels, etc.) designed to work together to aid digestion, especially of food.

Emotional (p. 38) *adj.*: relating to the expression of human feelings or sensibilities, such as joy, fear, happiness, sadness, etc.

Energy (p. 43) *n.*: power, motivated force; expressed in electromagnetic waves.

Environment (p. 37) *n.*: the circumstances, objects, or conditions by which one is surrounded; one's personal world or reality, as well as the collective world, or reality.

Essential (p. 29) *adj.*: of the utmost importance; important. Synonym: Fundamental.

Exist (p. 42) *v.*: of or pertaining to being; to have real being whether material or spiritual; to continue to be.

Fascinating (p. 22) *adj.*: commanding the interest of, compelling.

Fiber-optics (p. 25) *n.*: thin transparent fibers of glass or plastic through which light passes through for the purposes of lightning fast communication.

Fluid (p. 32) *n.*: a substance that tends to flow by nature; viscous.

Forgiving (p. 39) *v.*: to give up resentment of or claim to requital for a prior wrong.

Functions (p. 24) *n.*: the action for which a person or thing is specially fitted or used or for which a thing exists.

Gluteus Maximus (p. 28) *n.*: the outermost muscle of the three *glutei* (muscles) found in each of the human buttocks.

Identify (p. 36) *v.*: to establish the identity of one's self or others; or establish common identity with others.

Important (p. 35) *adj.*: marked by or indicative of significant worth, or consequence.

Ingredient (p. 33) *n.*: something that is included in a compound or is a component part of any combination or mixture.

Interpret (p. 23) *v.*: to explain or tell the meaning of; present in understandable terms; to conceive in the light of individual belief, judgment, or circumstance.

Meaning (p. 41) *n.*: the thing one intends to convey especially through language; the deeper *idea* that underlies or motivates one's actions.

Monitoring (p. 27) *v.*: to watch, keep track of, or check regularly, usually for a special purpose.

Muscles (p. 28) *n.*: tissues that help form, support and facilitate movement of the physical body.

Nervous System (p. 26) *n.*: the bodily system that, in vertebrates (such as all human beings), is made up of the brain and spinal cord, nerves, ganglia, and parts of the receptor organs and that receives and interprets stimuli and transmits impulses to the effector organs.

Network (p. 25) *n.*: an interconnected or interrelated chain, group, or system.

Obliged (p. 44) *adj.*: constrained and motivated by physical, moral, legal or ethical reason.

Parenthood (p. 35) *n.*: the state, condition, or standing of being a parent.

Pleasure (p. 38) *n.*: a source of delight or joy.

Pleasurable (p. 35) *adj.*: that which giving pleasure; delightful or joyful.

Pliable (p. 39) *adj.*: supple enough to bend freely or repeatedly without breaking; yielding readily, or easily.

Processes (p. 23) *n.*: describes a natural phenomenon marked by gradual changes that lead toward a particular result.

Proposition (p. 19) *n.*: something of an indicated kind; the objective meaning of a statement. (Gaining cooperation from people with such different beliefs is a tough *proposition.*)

Purpose (p. 37) *n.*: something set up as an object or end to be attained; a goal.

Region (p. 26) *n.*: any of the major subdivisions into which the body or one of its parts is divisible.

Relationships (p. 38) *n.*: the state of being related or interrelated; takes all forms including family, scholastic, business and romantic attachment.

Relevant (p. 44) *adj.*: having significant and demonstrable bearing on the matter at hand; importance and pertinence.

Respond (p. 23) *v.*: to say or do something in reply.

Sensations (p. 23) *n.*: immediate bodily stimulation (seeing, hearing, touches); awareness of.

Senses (p. 23) *n.*: the faculty of perceiving by means of sense organs (sight, hearing, taste, smell, touch).

Servant (p. 40) *n.*: one that performs duties about the person or home of a master or personal employer.

Skeleton (p. 29) *n.*: the bony framework that supports the soft tissues and protecting the internal organs of the human body.

Slightest (p. 27) *adj.*: smallest in kind or amount. Synonym: Itty bitty.

Spirit (p. 43) *n.*: an animating or vital principle held to give life to human beings; essence.

Status (p. 37) *n.*: the condition of a person or thing.

Somersaults (p. 30) n.: a leap or roll in which a person turns forward or backward in a complete revolution bringing the feet over the head and finally landing on the feet.

Temperature (p. 6) *n.*: degree of hotness or coldness measured on a definite scale; the degree of heat that is natural to the body of a living being.

Tissue (p. 29) *n.*: a cellular substance that forms one of the structural materials of the human body, such as the skin, and muscles.

Transports (p. 32) *v.*: transfers or conveys from one place to another.

Torso (p. 28) *n.*: the human trunk; the area below the neck and above the legs.

Touch (p. 2) *v.*: to bring a bodily part into contact with something or someone else, especially so as to perceive through the tactile sense.

Vital (p. 28) *adj.*: concerned with or necessary to the maintenance of life.

Wondrous (p. 39) *adj.*: that is to be marveled at.

52

Phaelos Order Form

Fax Orders: 310-214-2352. Send this form.

Postal Orders: Phaelos, Inc., Adam Abraham, P.O. Box 13523, Torrance, CA 90503, USA
Tel. 310-370-7211.

Please send the following books:

_____

_____

_____

Name:_____

Address:_____

City:_____ State:_____ Zip:_____

Telephone:_____

Email:_____

Sales Tax: Please add 8.25% for products shipped to California addresses.

Shipping by air:

US: $4 for the first title or item and $2 for each additional. International: $9 for the first title or item and $5 for each additional product.

Payment: ☐ Check ☐ Credit Card

☐ Visa ☐ Mastercard ☐ American Express

Card Number:_____Exp. Date:_____

Cardholder Name:_____